GLOBAL EVANGELISM SECRETS

■ ■ ■

End Time Tips

Prince Handley

University of Excellence Press

UNIVERSITY OF EXCELLENCE PRESS
Los Angeles ■ London ■ Tel Aviv

ISBN-13: 978-0692519691
ISBN-10: 0692519696

Printed in the USA

First Edition

■

The Social Media primer you need!

INTRODUCTION

The Gospel is not only cross-cultural—it is omni-cultural. There is always ONE benchmark to apprise whether we are effectively reaching any culture: **the cross-stake**.

In the world, and nations in particular, there are many cultures and sometimes micro cultures. Within each culture there are subcultures. Sometimes these subcultures overlap national and ethnic boundaries.

There are different **TRENDS** throughout the years and throughout your lifetime and ministry. There are different **TIMES** of refreshing as well as seasons of opportunity. There are different ministries as well as gifts of the Holy Spirit—but only **ONE LORD.**

This book is a primer for social media evangelism and is designed to give the reader examples of trends in media, generational cultures and suggestions for practical outreach.

It is not designed to replace what you may be doing, but to provide NEW ideas through practical examples and suggestions.

Resources are also included to help the reader help others!

Especially helpful to the person engaged in Global Evangelism and Church Planting are **tips pertaining to protection and power** while you are working on special projects for the LORD.

For advanced missions strategies the reader should consult the following two books by Prince Handley:

The Art of Christian Warfare

New Global Strategy

GLOBAL EVANGELISM SECRETS

■ ■ ■

End Time Tips

God is eternally young. He is NOT some old man with a long beard sitting in a rocking chair!

The Gospel is not only cross-cultural—it is omni-cultural. There is always ONE benchmark to apprise whether we are effectively reaching any culture: **the cross-stake**.

One time, after preaching to the usual mega audience, Billy Graham felt discouraged because he sensed a lack of power during the message. A close associate told him, "Billy, you forgot the cross!"

In the world, and nations in particular, there are many cultures and sometimes micro cultures. Within each culture there are subcultures. Sometimes these subcultures overlap national and ethnic boundaries. For example, age stratification: a specific example of which would be youth. The micro cultures within these sub cultures constantly change; some over long periods of time, usually in less civilized, less advanced societies.

TRENDS

An example of a micro culture would be the age groups in Western and some European cultures labeled Generation "Y" (or those attempting to emulate them). Baby Boomers were born in the post WW II years of 1946 thru 1955, with a later generation from 1955 through 1965 referred to as Generation Jones (which was the first wave of Generation Y). They are also referred to as the Echo Generation or Millennium Generation.

Generation X'ers were born after the Post WW II baby boom, from the early 1960's through early 1980's.

Generation Y, also known as the Milllennials were born somewhere between the early 1980's through the early 2,000's. However Generation Y is extremely different. Many are from single parent families, or from families with two working parents—or a grandparent who is taking care of them. As a result they are usually financially responsible and more independent.

Generation Y spends more on consumer goods than Generation X, and because of their numbers, are the targets of major marketing strategies. They are STIMULATED by more information, and more options, and situations that require decision making. They are often accused of growing up too fast. What a PERFECT segment of society to reach with the message of the CROSS and then train to reach the world in these days before the return of Messiah.

GEN 13 (also referred to as The Millennials) define a core of beliefs as to life style and generally fall into the age group of 25 to 35 (during 2014 through 2017). **Many in this group grew up in their grandparents homes as a result of their parents' divorce**. They know how to make a fast decision based upon pragmatics, especially in the area of economics and money—but can easily perceive the truth and value of the Good News when presented to them with love and sincerity. **Prince Handley believes this is a KEY segment to evangelize for entry into the Last Days.**

Also, Prince Handley believes the greatest segment to evangelize NOW and in the future is under 15 years of age. The mass of the population (over 50 percent) in nations is under the age of 15. If you reach the young people, you will effectively:

1. Reach the next generation and future leaders;

2. Reach those who will have the longest lifetime of service for the LORD.

3. Reach the greatest amount of people.

NOTE: Use the **Wordless Book** found here: http://www.realmiracles.org/wordless-books.html

TIMES

Sometimes culturally diverse societies have a commonality of access. For example, the Internet. As oppressive countries like Iran, China, North Korea and Islamic nations find that Internet access is NOT optional if they want to do business in the global market, they have begun bringing the Internet into their geopolitical borders. Countries like China try to control free

9

speech and thought on the Internet but that's like trying to hide sugar from ants.

Dictators who have tried to control the dissemination of information via the Internet have NOT developed an effective counter measure—and are NOT likely to do so. There are too many smart kids who can drive the "bad guys" crazier! Check out Prince Handley's **Key for End Time Super Hacking and Cyber Warfare** at: www.uofe.org. Select tab at left titled "NBC & BIO WARFARE."

The technology gap between keeping the Internet out of an oppressive regime and that regime surviving well in the global market is fast closing.

Check this out. The Internet is ridiculed for its ability to quickly disseminate a "lie"—consider all the Spam hoax emails you've received. As helplessly as we try to eliminate Spam, so oppressive governments will NOT be able to "filter" out the TRUTH! Another PERFECT segment of society to reach with the message of the CROSS and then train to reach the world in these days before the return of Messiah. Think about it—and I suggest: ACT EXPEDITIOUSLY!

SUGGESTIONS TO ADD TO YOUR GAME

1. SEND EMAIL TO GOVERNMENT, TRADE, AND UNIVERSITY OFFICES ALL OVER THE WORLD TELLING THEM ABOUT THE WEBSITE AT WWW.UOFE.ORG

FOR EMAIL ADDRESSES, LOOK IN TRADE JOURNALS, MAGAZINES, OR NEWSPAPERS. THE INTERNET IS ALSO A GOOD SOURCE. YOU MAY RECEIVE EMAIL ADDRESSES THAT ARE SENT TO YOUR WORK OR HOME, ALSO, THAT YOU MAY REPLY TO. NOBODY IS GOING TO BITE YOU. PLUS, YOU DON'T KNOW WHO IS GOING TO READ THE EMAIL ON THE OTHER END: IT MAY BE A SECRETARY—OR THE OWNER OF A BUSINESS—WHO IS READY TO COMMIT SUICIDE OR GIVE UP ON LIFE. IT MAY ALSO BE THE NEXT GREAT END TIME PROPHET! USE YOUR FAITH. ***DON'T BE AFRAID TO "COLOR OUTSIDE THE LINES!"***

SUGGESTION: SEARCH FOR EMAIL ADDRESSES OF COMPANIES WHICH ARE BASED INSIDE ISRAEL.

MAKE THE EMAIL MESSAGE—OR, THE REPLY—SHORT. YOU MAY WANT TO USE **YOUR OWN WEBSITE ADDRESS**; HOWEVER, **WE HAVE INCLUDED THE SITES AND EMAILS IN THESE 7 EXAMPLES IN CASE YOU DO NOT HAVE ONE**.

2. IF YOU DO A SUBSEQUENT EMAIL TO AREAS WHERE THERE MAY BE A CHRISTIAN ELEMENT THEN TELL THEM ABOUT "THE APOSTLES NEWSLETTER." THEY MAY SUBSCRIBE HERE: PRINCEHANDLEY@GMAIL.COM

3. OF COURSE, DON'T DO ANYTHING ILLEGAL, AND FOR SURE DON'T SEND "SPAM MAIL."

4. YOU SHOULD ALWAYS GIVE RECIPIENTS AN OPPORTUNITY TO "OPT OUT" AT THE END OF THE EMAIL BY PROVIDING THEM AN "UNSUBSCRIBE" EMAIL ADDRESS, EVEN IF YOU'RE ONLY SENDING THE EMAIL ONE TIME.

5. IF YOU RECEIVE A REPLY ASKING FOR PRAYER OR SPIRITUAL HELP AND YOU DON'T KNOW HOW TO ANSWER, THEN GO TO THE "SEARCH" BUTTON AT THE RIGHT OF THE WEBSITE APOSTLE.LIBSYN.COM AND FIND YOUR ANSWER. FOR EXAMPLE, IF THEY ASK YOU A QUESTION ABOUT ANTICHRIST, JUST TYPE IN THE WORD "ANTICHRIST" IN OUR SEARCH SECTION. USUALLY YOU WILL HAVE SEVERAL ANSWERS TO CHOOSE FROM. SELECT THE ONE YOU LIKE, COPY IT AND PASTE IT INTO AN EMAIL TO SEND THEM AN ANSWER.

6. HERE ARE THREE (3) EXAMPLES OF SHORT, BUT EFFECTIVE EMAILS:

>>> MIRACLES, HEALING, PRAYER, AND HELP FOR YOU: WWW.HEALING.LIBSYN.COM

>>> STRATEGIES FOR LIVING IN THE LAST DAYS: WWW.UOFE.ORG

>>> 1,000'S OF FREE RESOURCES FOR YOU: WWW.REALMIRACLES.ORG

7. TAKE ADVANTAGE OF SOCIAL MEDIA: MYSPACE, YOUTUBE, FACEBOOK, LINKEDIN, TWITTER AND OTHERS. DIRECT THEM TO: WWW.TWITTER.COM/PRINCEHANDLEY

WHAT NOT TO DO ON SOCIAL MEDIA

Following are some "tips" gleaned from Randi Zuckerberg (sister of Facebook founder, Mark Zuckerberg) that she shared at *ClickZ Live New York* about **what NOT to do on social media**.

Vague posts

Humble bragger

13

Don't be a #hash #hole

Obsessive food blogger

Over-filtered Instagrammer

Romantic public exchanges

The old person who just doesn't get it

NOTE: Growing your brand with **great (helpful) content** is the number one most valuable thing you can do for your followers.

NEW TRENDS

Cars are a growing internet enabled "device" that will get a lot more development in the coming years. My 2016 model has three (3) charging devices. (My 1991 Camaro convertible that I bought NEW has none. What does that tell you!?) HINT: You may want to use some audio.

Also, wearable internet devices are—and will become—more fashionable. So, plan and implement with these new trends in mind.

If you have an IDEA or an APP that you need help developing, here are some resources for you. **Custom Made** is a community that can connect **your idea** with people that can make it happen. Creating an app is like being a maker. **App Builder** is a tool to make it easy to create **your app**.

Images are proven to be more effective and inspire significantly greater engagement on social content. **Getty has released 35 million images for FREE**. Why not promote not only your posts—but also your followers from time to time—with images and photos. The Samsung Galaxy "S6" smart phone has boss photo effects as well as video enhancements.

SUGGESTIONS:

1. Think of ways to make it easier for people to do what they want to while learning about Jesus.

2. Do a "digital" Sabbath one day a week. Cut yourself loose from devices, TV, computers ... even phones.

TONGUES

For creativity, power, wisdom and direction pray in the Spirit. The Holy Spirit knows HOW to reach the cultures and micro cultures. He is their Creator! Also, the Spirit of God will anoint your projects. The Bible tells us, *"Not by power nor by might, but by my Spirit says the Lord."* The Baptism in the Holy Spirit may provide a person with a **special spirit of ability or talent**, such as:

> A spirit of craftsmanship;
> A spirit of music;
> A spirit of art;
> A spirit of creativity.

In Exodus 31, verses 1-11, a man named Bezaleel was filled with the Spirit of God in wisdom, and in understanding, and in

16

knowledge and in all manner of workmanship. He was enabled by the Spirit to work in gold, silver, and brass; in cutting and setting stones, and in carving wood: to help in the building of the tabernacle. Another example—about 500 years later, King David said that the pattern of the temple which his son, Solomon, built was **given to David "by the Spirit."** *"All this,"* said David, *"the Lord made me understand in writing by his hand upon me, even all the works of this pattern."* [I Chronicles 28:12-19]

Many times you will also need protection as you work on projects the LORD assigns you.

I knew of a high school teacher who was a wonderful witness for the Jesus Christ. One day a group of students who were Satanists or witches had a curse placed on a recording. They called the teacher on his telephone to play the recording to him. Before the teacher answered the phone, the Spirit impressed him to speak in tongues when he answered the phone. **The teacher obeyed the Holy Spirit—spoke in**

17

tongues—and the recording device (the player) on the other end of the line blew up (exploded). The next day at school this group of students told him they wanted what he had (about 10 of them as I remember) and he prayed with them to receive Christ!

In a school of ministry where I was Dean, the host pastor related a story of a Christian girl who was abducted by a group of young men. They took her in a car with the intent of raping her. The girl was a Christian, from a Christian home. Her parents were Spirit-filled; however, she had never received the Baptism of the Holy Spirit. Suddenly she decided it might help if she had this Power. She prayed to be baptized in the Spirit. **When the Holy Spirit came upon her, she spoke in tongues. The young men let her out of the car unharmed**.

I prayed for an aunt of mine who was in the hospital more than 1,000 miles away. I had not seen her in years. I did NOT know what was wrong with her; only that the Lord told me to call her and pray for her in tongues. I did NOT know but she had an abdominal cancer as big as a person's fist and was to have surgery the next day. **When I prayed for her in tongues—the language of the Spirit—the cancer dissolved (disappeared) and she was healed instantly and did NOT have to have the surgery. Praise God!**

A good friend of mine, John Garlock, was raised as an MK (missionary kid) in Africa. His father, H. B. Garlock was a tremendous man of God and wrote a book named *Before They Kill and Eat You*. You may special order it at any most Christian book stores or from CFNI (Christ for the Nations Institute) in Dallas, Texas USA. Deep in the interior of a jungle region he encountered a tribe who had tied a native to a stake or tree and was **preparing to burn him alive**.

The elder Garlock attempted to intercede for the man, pleading with the tribal leaders to let the man go and have mercy on him. His plans failed and they **then tied up Garlock next to the native, preparing to burn them both**. Garlock prayed and began to speak in tongues—the language of the Spirit. Whatever the Holy Spirit uttered through him so scared the attackers that they ran away and left the men unharmed.

The Holy Spirit will also **guide you** as well as anoint you for creativity, power and wisdom. Jesus said, *"He [The Comforter] will guide you into all truth"* ... AND ... *"He will show you things to come."* **The Spirit will not only guide you into spiritual and scriptural truth—especially the knowledge of salvation in Jesus the Messiah—but He will guide you into truth and protect you from deception in earthly matters if you seek Him and wait on Him**. He will show you things to come—not only in spiritual and scriptural issues—but also in your life ... many times warning you ahead of time of impending danger or an unwise move if you seek Him and wait on Him.

The Apostle Paul received a prophecy NOT to go up to Jerusalem, but He did because the Spirit led him to. Another time he attempted to go into areas that he was constrained by the Spirit to NOT enter ... until the Spirit directed him to another place where God wanted him. **Let God's Spirit guide you in the projects and fields of labor where HE wants you.** He knows what is BEST for you and the people to which you are to minister!

SUMMARY

There are different **TRENDS** throughout the years and throughout your lifetime and ministry. There are different **TIMES** of refreshing as well as seasons of opportunity. There are different ministries as well as gifts of the Holy Spirit—but only **ONE LORD**. Appropriate what He has made available to you—pray in **TONGUES** for direction—and never forget to communicate the **MESSAGE of the CROSS** which is the **POWER** of God unto salvation!

21

OPPORTUNITY TO PARTICIPATE

You can reach LOTS of people for Christ by doing a "Review" on Amazon about these two books: **New Global Strategy** and **The Art of Christian Warfare.**

The Art of Christian Warfare is a companion book to **New Global Strategy.** It is much more focused on church planting and building disciples—and also includes "tips and suggestions" for the Christian worker: on and off the field.

NOTE 1: New Global Strategy is ONLY available in e-Book format because there are LOTS of links (probably weeks of study in it) to help train the Christian mission director or worker. (Less pages - 37 - but lots of links).

NOTE 2: The Art of Christian Warfare is a manual and guide for global missions: it will get the job finished. **See the contents**. This book has the LARGEST amount of **free** pages view (for a book of this size) of any book I have ever seen on Amazon. It is 95 pages and available in both e-Book and Print format.

A Review for both books will be appreciated. These books will effectively prepare Christian workers for global outreach in the last days. **Thanks for your help!**

P.S. - We did a perusal of the available books on "Missions" online and they are generally too long AND too expensive.

Your friend,
Prince Handley

UNIVERSITY OF EXCELLENCE PRESS
Los Angeles ▪ London ▪ Tel Aviv

NOTE

We listen to our readers. Tell us what **new**
subject matter you would like to see published.
Email your ideas to:
universityofexcellence@gmail.com

OTHER BOOKS BY PRINCE HANDLEY

- Map of the End Times
- How to Do Great Works
- Flow Chart of Revelation
- Action Keys for Success
- Health and Healing Complete Guide to Wholeness
- Prophetic Calendar for Israel & Nations: Thru 2023
- Healing Deliverance
- How to Receive God's Power with Gifts of the Spirit
- Healing for Mental and Physical Abuse
- Victory Over Opposition and Resistance
- Healing of Emotional Wounds
- How to Be Healed and Live in Divine Health
- Healing from Fear, Shame and Anger
- How to Receive Healing and Bring Healing to Others
- New Global Strategy: Enabling Missions
- The Art of Christian Warfare
- Success Cycles and Secrets
- New Testament Bible Studies (A Study Manual)
- Babylon the Bitch – Enemy of Israel
- Resurrection Multiplication – Miracle Production
- Faith and Quantum Physics – Your Future
- Conflict Healing – Relational Health
- Decision Making 101 – Know for Sure
- Total Person Toolbox
- Prophecy, Transition & Miracles
- Enhanced Humans – Mystery Matrix
- The "Spiritual Growth" Series (several volumes)

AVAILABLE AT AMAZON AND OTHER BOOK STORES

Prince Handley Books

http://www.realmiracles.org/books.html

UNIVERSITY OF EXCELLENCE PRESS

Los Angeles ■ London ■ Tel Aviv

www.ingramcontent.com/pod-product-compliance
Lightning Source LLC
Chambersburg PA
CBHW060607030426
42337CB00019B/3650